the spiritual journey of:

....

(name)

....

(month / day / year)

Destination: A happier you.

invitation to happiness

7 inspirations from your inner angel

RYUHO OKAWA

IRH PRESS

RO Books is a registered trademark of IRH Press Co., Ltd.

IRH PRESS

New York • Tokyo

Distributed by Midpoint Trade Books. www.midpointtrade.com

Library of Congress Cataloging-in-Publication Data

ISBN 13: 978-1-942125-01-3

ISBN 10: 1-942125-01-1

Printed in China
First edition

DESIGNER: Karla Baker
Cover/Interior Image © Jan Engel/Fotolia

contents

list of exercises

an invitation from your inner angel

This book is your personal invitation to a spiritual journey guided by your inner angel. Each of us has one, and yours is your guide to spiritual happiness. The purpose of this book is to help you find your joy by connecting with that inner voice, spirit, soul, or higher self. There's material to contemplate and an area to journal your inspirations and discoveries about the book's seven themes. To begin your journey to a new level of happiness, you need merely to accept your invitation and turn the pages.

YOUR INNER ANGEL:
YOUR SOUL AND GUIDE

There are rare moments in life when just the right answer or idea comes to us from out of nowhere at just the right time. It may be an inspiration about which path to take in life or a hint for developing a new business. Sometimes a solution presents itself when we're faced with a difficult decision and questioning our choices. The voice or words come from within or appear before us as if they fell from heaven—and sometimes they come from the most unexpected people. These are the moments when we intuitively know, "That's it." Each instance is evidence that we are never really alone. There's a spiritual existence that supports each of us, guides us, and stands beside us in life.

This spiritual existence is your *inner angel* or *guardian*

spirit. Your inner angel is not a completely separate being but actually a part of your soul. You can also call this spiritual existence your *subconscious*. The consciousness of your physical self does not represent all of your soul but only a part of it. The rest of your soul remains in the other world as the subconscious. Just as a flower is made up of several petals, your soul is made up of six individual energies. You, the person living on earth now, are like one petal of a flower. Your inner angel guides and protects you from heaven as another petal of the flower that makes up your soul. Your soul is much more than the energy that resides in your physical body: it is your infinite source of power and is connected to a vast energy with great wisdom.

No matter how lonely we may feel, our angels are always trying to support us, help us, and encourage us from heaven. When we face difficulties, hardships, and pain, they are there for inspiration, guidance, and protection. When we stand at an important crossroad, our inner angels lead us to the right path. And knowingly or not, we are continually embraced, nurtured, and sustained by this magnificent force of love.

RECEIVING HELP
FROM YOUR ANGEL

We all face difficult or unfortunate situations in life, and hard times make some people wonder whether it's true that angels are always protecting and guiding us, or even whether they exist at all.

Life in this world is every soul's opportunity for development, and each one of us is responsible for learning from our experiences. This is why heavenly spirits are not allowed to take complete control over our lives and live them on behalf, as if we were only puppets. We all have to lead our own lives, but our angels also do whatever they can to influence things to our advantage. Your guardian angel helps you by sending inspiration at important turning points in your life.

Say there is an opening for a managerial position in a company, and two qualified people are competing against each other for this position.

Their guardian angels will both do everything they can to help them get the position. They will, for example, send inspiration to convince the personnel director that the person they are guiding is suitable for the position. Or if you fall in love with someone that you think is your ideal marriage partner, your guardian angel will work very hard to attract that person and bring the two of you together.

Your inner angel guides and protects you throughout your life. Knowing this will increase your awareness of the help you receive from heaven. Your inner angel may protect you by getting someone to block your way to keep you from taking the wrong path in life and to push you toward your right path. The most important thing is to always believe. Believe that your angel will guide you to the right path and open up a way for you to pursue it.

inner angel memories

What memorable moments, inspirations, ideas, or thoughts have come to you from a source within that you recognized as knowing or spiritual?

....
....
....
....
....
....
....
....

Remember the turning points in your life. In what critical moments have you experienced guidance? Make a list of these moments.

✳ ....
✳ ....
✳ ....
✳ ....
✳ ....
✳ ....
✳ ....
✳ ....
✳ ....
✳ ....

When you have faced difficulties or been at a standstill, how have you been guided to make the right decisions? Describe a memorable moment.

THE SOURCE OF YOUR INSPIRATION

Guardian spirits are neither omniscient nor omnipotent, nor does their awareness differ greatly from our own. But they do have a higher perspective than their counterparts on earth, and they are the source of our insights and inspirations. Your angel can often foresee what will happen to you and help you move your life forward. So the first step toward a life of happiness is to remain open to the guidance you receive from within.

Your inner angel also cherishes your efforts to open up a path on your own. By maintaining high aspirations, dedication, perseverance, selflessness, and humility, you can strengthen your link to a higher awareness. So when the door to your future finally opens, give thanks to the heavenly spirit who assisted you. The stronger and more lasting your gratitude is, the more love and support you will receive.

thanking your inner angel

Write a thank-you note to your inner guide, voice, or angel for all the guidance, inspiration, and protection you have received.

Dear inner angel,

....
....
....
....
....
....
....
....
....
....
....
....
....
....
....
....
....
....
....
....

a calm mind

the perfect beginning

To find joy, find your inner peace.
When you learn to live with a
steady, calm, unreactive mind,
your stillness will reflect the
world, other people, and—
above all—who you truly are.

HARMONY OF THE MIND:
THE PATH TO SPIRITUAL FREEDOM

Living here on earth in a physical form makes it easy to forget our innate spiritual freedom. But by harmonizing our minds with the vibrations of heaven, we can connect with our truest selves and remember what it is like to have a spiritual freedom.

We all send and receive various vibrational frequencies throughout our days. The thoughts that dominate our minds heavily influence the types of energy we receive from others, as well as the energies we reflect out into the world. Each of us has felt the distress, anger, or hopelessness of another. These feelings are like magnets whose coarse vibrations attract more of the same types of emotions. A calm mind boosts the serenity of our vibrations, inviting that same peaceful energy to be reflected back to us from those around us.

The first step toward achieving serenity within is to practice detachment. Practicing letting go of all of your distracting thoughts calms your mind and allows your vibration to resonate with the vibration of the higher world. A repeated practice of cutting off the worldly vibrations that surround you and looking within will help you achieve a deeper tranquility and reach your most spiritual self.

happy truth

Life in this world is like a deep-sea dive, and your body is like your diving suit. The journey is dangerous and difficult. The water is cold, and the bottom of the ocean is dark. You may get washed away by a current and encounter creatures of the sea. You need a diving suit to block the coldness of the water, fins on your feet to swim, a snorkel and an oxygen tank to breathe, and swimming goggles to see. But because of this equipment, you may feel confined and lose your sense of freedom.

CREATING YOUR SANCTUARY

The first step toward calming your mind is to create a place where you will not be influenced by worldly vibrations. Choose a quiet, private space where you will not be interrupted. Avoid a room where the phone might ring or other people might come in. Shutting out outside influences makes it easier for you to isolate yourself from the disturbing vibrations, emotions, and thoughts of other people and from the everyday matters that trouble your mind. Create an area where you feel quiet and relaxed, as if you are sitting on a mountaintop or lying on a beach.

RELAXED BODY, RELAXED MIND

Quiet and calm breathing can relax your body, help free you from the distraction of the world's vibrations, and attune to the infinite world beyond. With practice, the breathing techniques described here can bring tranquility and a sense of contentment—evidence that you're on a path to your most spiritual self. Regular practice may even leave you flooded with a heavenly light of warmth and joy.

Mindful and relaxed breathing also has numerous practical benefits. As oxygen-rich blood circulates through your body and brain, your heart rate and brain waves become calm. Regulating your physical rhythms quiets your vibrations in the world, freeing you from the worries and stress of everyday life.

Your mind and your body are one. Relaxing your body leads to a relaxed mind, so sit in a comfortable position. You don't need to be in a typical meditational posture (cross-legged or kneeling). Any posture or style that allows you to sit and concentrate for a while is fine. If possible, sit with a straight spine to help you stay awake and alert.

Turning the palms up on your knees makes it easier for you to turn off part of the mind, feel a sense of liberation from worldly issues, and find comfort in where you are. Turning your palms facing down puts the mind in a more active or dynamic state and helps you concentrate your thoughts on a specific vision. Joining your hands in prayer helps you communicate with heaven. Your hands transmit specific signals that reach the spirits that correspond to the messages you send out.

deep-breathing exercise

1   Sit in a comfortable position with your palms upward on your knees in the sanctuary you've created for peace and contemplation or an area where you feel comfortable and will not get distracted.

2   Breathe in and exhale slowly. Inhale deeply through the nose and chest. Visualize the breath reaching the lower abdomen. Then exhale quietly and slowly through the mouth. As you breathe, visualize the fresh blood and oxygen circulating throughout your entire body—your head, neck, shoulders, hips, etc. This will harmonize the vibrations in your mind and body.

3   Imagine pouring muddy water into a cup and stirring it up. When the cup is still, the water rises to the top above the mud. Imagine your mind in the same way: clouded by thoughts but clearing with every breath until it is tranquil and transparent.

DOWNLOADABLE
MUSIC AVAILABLE AT
OKAWABOOKS.COM

angel tip

Your physical condition has a significant impact on your spiritual health. To get the best results from your contemplation exercises:

1 *If you're exhausted, rest and restore your physical strength.*

2 *To make sure you're influenced only by positive spirits, refrain from drinking alcohol before doing any type of contemplation, meditation, or visualization.*

3 *Boost your concentration and mood through regular exercise.*

QUIETING CHATTER
IN THE MIND

Each of us faces conflict with others at some point, and sometimes we regret our actions or words. But with a mindfulness practice of breathing and contemplation, we can gain control over how we react to the things that disturb us, whether they come from within or without.

Regular practice of calming the mind quiets the constant ripples of thoughts and emotions that cause stress. Our ability to calm our mind determines whether the ripples of our lives are big storms on the ocean or small pebbles tossed into a lake.

TRY THIS OUT
ON THE NEXT PAGE

freeing your mind from worries

1   Sit in stillness, and review your day. Release your tension and allow your thoughts to come up.

2   Ask yourself whether any words, expressions, or actions—from other people or yourself—troubled your mind today. List them here:

* ....
* ....
* ....
* ....
* ....
* ....
* ....
* ....
* ....
* ....
* ....
* ....
* ....
* ....
* ....
* ....

3   *Looking over your list, what was it that most disrupted your inner peace today?*

....
....
....
....
....
....
....
....
....
....
....
....
....
....
....
....
....
....
....
....
....

4   *When our minds are disturbed, there's always a cause. Once
you know what's causing you to feel uneasy, consider why it's
making you suffer so much. Did it happen because of what
you said or did? Did you play a part in what happened, either
directly or indirectly?*

5   *If you think that you are responsible for what happened, either directly or indirectly, ponder what you could have done and contemplate the lesson you learned. You can regain peace of mind when you see these experiences as opportunities to learn. These empowering practices can calm the chatter in your head.*

....
....
....
....
....
....
....
....
....
....
....
....
....
....
....
....
....
....

If you are especially troubled by relationships with others, see chapter 5 Forgiveness.

angel tip

In stillness, we find joy. When you are unable
to find peace of mind, say this prayer out loud:

"I am at peace. My mind is in a tranquil state.
I am moving forward serenely as I work to
improve myself every day."

FEEL THE LIGHT.
GET INSPIRED.

Your surface consciousness often gets cluttered with worldly thoughts, but by contemplating your words, actions, and thoughts, you can clean your mind. A calm and clean mind is essential to receiving inspirations and guidance from your inner angel.

When we are aligned with our inner angels, it becomes intuitive to make the right decisions and discern which direction to take in life. When we face major life decisions about things like career, love, and relationships, we're able to sense when something is true for us and when it is not. We begin to receive inspirations about the decisions we should make to walk on the right path.

As you continue cleaning and concentrating your mind regularly, there will be moments when you are in tune with your inner angel. The bliss you feel will be beyond words. The daily support, encouragement, and sense of security you gain will allow you to find a new level of happiness. And the gratitude you will feel will naturally make you want to reflect your happiness outward and share it with everyone around you.

Introspective contemplation offers a precious opportunity to connect to your truest self and experience a glimpse of an even higher spiritual world. With this inner connection, you will be able to transform the light you receive into a source of vitality and energy you can use to live a more meaningful and positive life.

By calming your mind and

looking within, you'll find your right path and a zest for living. Your zest for life will be an ever-flowing source of spiritual energy you will draw on to spread happiness in the world.

You will also be able to refine your mind and regain your original self so that you can start living a life filled with light, hope, and happiness.

the true you

awakening to your divine nature

When we truly believe that divine nature has always been within us, we become empowered with the hope and strength we need to offer our gifts to the world. The journey of finding your unique purpose and making it bloom in your own way will pave the way to your happiness.

RARE.
PRECIOUS.
YOU.

Each of us has infinite potential to bring the gifts of our divine nature to the world. The more we reveal this part of our true selves, the more we are able to create happiness for ourselves and everyone around us. It's important to remember that this real you has always been there, beneath any of the distracting layers that could be hiding it. And you have the power to bring it out.

What is it that keeps us from believing in this diamond-like self inside us? Usually it is past disappointments that have continued to weigh on us. But nothing that has happened in the past can ever make our divine nature disappear. When we begin to believe in our divine nature and start living

as our true selves, we shine. There's no limit to the brightness we can reach. And as we feel ourselves beginning to shine, we gain the courage to keep going. The key is to look within and search out our divine nature.

Like diamonds, our true selves reflect a multitude of heavenly facets: love, knowledge, courage, light, wisdom, justice, and compassion. The purpose of our lives is to search out, grow, and actualize as many of these qualities as possible. Everyone is on this spiritual journey to attain eternal growth. Each of us has some facets that are more polished than others, and our aim is to create a beautiful balance between all of the facets within us.

Contemplation and introspection are excellent tools for finding our heavenly attributes and connecting to our true selves. The goal of contemplation is not to put ourselves down for our faults or weaknesses but to discover the good that is already within us. When we get caught up in disappointments, we develop a negative self-image or a pattern of self-blame that doesn't serve us. This can happen when we lose hope as a result of overwhelming challenges such as illness, job loss, or heartbreak. So when we start believing that we're not good enough or become anxious about what others think of us, it's important to remember that these thoughts and feelings are simply signs that we need to take a step back and reconnect with our true selves. So when you find yourself easily disheartened, know that your true nature is much stronger than you believe and that you have far more potential than you've yet achieved.

visualizing your true self

Humans have always had the power to receive heavenly inspirations. The more we're able to let them in, the more connected we become with our true selves, and the more we will have to offer the world. Visualization and contemplation are simple, practical tools that anyone can practice daily to grow spiritually.

1   *Begin by closing your eyes and sitting in stillness.*

2   *Visualize your true self within you, sparkling as splendidly as a diamond.*

3   *See your body being filled with golden light from heaven.*

4   *Watch the light fill your heart, making the darkness vanish as it grows and grows.*

5   *Feel the warmth from the light.*

Continue this visualization until your heart feels warmer, lighter, and renewed and you can see yourself as a wonderful person, shining with kindness.

DOWNLOADABLE
MUSIC AVAILABLE AT
OKAWABOOKS.COM

TRUE VS. FALSE SELF

Through contemplation, the thoughts and mindsets that oppose our divine nature will gradually and naturally become more visible and approachable. If you discover thoughts within yourself that shine with the light of your true self, let go of the thoughts that oppose them. For example, if you discover the characteristic of love within yourself, then let go of your feelings of hatred. If you visualize yourself blessing other people, remove jealousy from your mind. If gratitude wells up from within, get rid of sarcastic and malicious remarks. If you can feel peace in your mind, get rid of impatience and irritation. If you visualize a healthy romantic relationship, you should refrain from purely physical relationships. If you feel a pure, tranquil mind that is free from uncontrollable desires, let go of negative, troubled thoughts. This is how we can keep polishing and shining our diamond within.

It can be difficult to reflect on ten years or even one year all at once, so the key is to develop a habit of daily contemplation. Try taking ten or fifteen minutes before bed to review that day's thoughts, feelings, actions, and conversations. Ask yourself which of these moments best represented your true self and in which moments you may have given in to a false self. This simple practice of mindfulness powerfully reconnects us with gratitude. We feel deeply grateful for all the things we have been given and all the love we've received. We remember how much our friends and family have believed in us and all our hopes and dreams. It's a spiritual renewal that moves us forward from mistakes of the past. Sometimes with joy, and sometimes with healing tears, this practice rejuvenates us with the power to make a fresh, new start every day.

two sides of you

Make a practice of reconnecting with your true self by taking ten to fifteen minutes daily to remember your conversations and actions from throughout the day.

The actions your true self took: Which actions or words, if any, do you feel came from your divine nature? What did you say or do that feels as though it may have represented a heavenly attribute?

....

....

....

....

....

....

....

....

....

....

....

....

....

....

....

....

....

....

The actions your false self took: Which actions or words, if any, do you feel did not come from your true self?

....
....
....
....
....
....
....
....
....
....

How will you make a fresh, new start today?

....
....
....
....
....
....
....
....
....
....

TAKE PRIDE IN YOUR STRENGTHS

Remembering that we have divine nature can be especially challenging in vulnerable times of sorrow and adversity. Our past often haunts us with our faults, our mistakes, and the things we "should've" or "could've" done. We spiral downward and have trouble believing in ourselves. In these moments, it helps to remember that no matter what kind of past any of us has had, there's a part of us that did all we could and remained true to our heart. There's always something in us that we can be proud of—for example, we can be proud of the effort we've made to live as honestly and sincerely as we could.

Our strengths are also something to be proud of. Each of our strengths is a wonderfully unique part of us that gives off a characteristic shine and color based on how we've worked to reveal it. Some of us are natural educators, while others are politicians or entrepreneurs.

Sometimes we develop a sense of inferiority when we notice our uniqueness, because we compare ourselves with others and notice only our weaknesses. In reality, our differences from others are signs that our souls are made of different strengths and characteristics. Or sometimes, becoming aware of a weakness simply means that we've discovered a new possibility for self-betterment.

Contemplating your strengths is especially powerful in times of failure or disappointment, because these events often either reveal our greatest strengths to us or show us how we haven't been living by our divine nature. They are valuable opportunities for us to get rid of our false sense of self, and, above all, they prove to us the resilient strength of our innate worth against the greatest of setbacks and adversities. Nothing can destroy our divine nature.

finding your strengths

List three of your greatest strengths below. If you have difficulty thinking of what your strengths might be, consider the positive things others have said about you, and look within for your own personal insights about what you like about yourself.

Examples: Love, consideration, kindness, courage, wisdom, honesty, diligence, a peaceful mind, a blessing heart, gratitude, cheerfulness, effort, faith, prayer, affluence, generosity, a mind free from attachments, a habit of speaking positively, sympathy, justice, high aspirations, personal growth, success at creating a healthy relationship or harmony within the family, patience, an unshakable mind, a strong will, hope, benevolence.

1 ....
....
....
....

2 ....
....
....
....

3 ....
....
....
....
....

Closing your eyes, recall a time when you acted from any of these strengths.

....
....
....
....
....
....
....
....
....
....

Name some of the areas you hope to work on that aren't yet strengths.

....
....
....
....
....
....
....
....
....
....

Closing your eyes, visualize a specific situation in which you act with strength in an area in which you usually think of yourself as weak.

UNIQUELY
YOU

Our differences often cause friction and distress. But they also inspire great wonder, learning, and pleasure. They're why we enjoy being around one another so much. And when we unite our different talents, possibilities expand infinitely, and we achieve many feats. Sharing our unique gifts helps us learn, teach, motivate, and help one another. We are all supposed to be different, because it is this abundant variety that makes our life in this world so interesting. It is our varied and unique purposes that allow us to develop spiritually, both individually and together.

When we compare ourselves with others, we often lose sight of our most important truth: the universe holds a unique place for each of us.

Everyone has a special place that's right for them. And if you're on the path to living out your potential in your best life, happiness will follow not only for you but for others as well. When you stay true to yourself and remember how important your role in the world is, you keep in touch with your purpose in life and know how to make best use of your potential to fulfill your sense of purpose.

To discover your unique gifts, consider what area or subject you find most intriguing. Your strong interest shows your hidden talent. You bring out your best when you devote yourself to something that fascinates you. Whatever fascinates you—a sport, an area of study, a form of art, or a hobby—put effort into it for three years, and you will find a new confidence. Once you have reached a certain level in one field, you can move on to another field and keep expanding your horizons. It takes patience and effort to develop a new skill or learn something different, and you may not see immediate results. But your efforts will pay off some day. As long as you keep moving forward, you will one day be rewarded with joy for never having given up on cultivating your innate gifts.

finding your unique gifts

Contemplate your unique gifts and the role you have taken in this lifetime. When you discover your unique purpose, you will know how to bring your gifts to the world, and you will shine.

What would you love to learn more than anything? What gives you most joy and fulfillment?

....
....
....
....
....
....
....
....
....
....
....
....
....
....
....
....
....

In what situations do you find yourself shining?

....

....

....

....

....

....

....

....

....

What captivates your soul? What do you think are the unique talents you were born with?

....

....

....

....

....

....

....

....

....

What kind of role do you think you play in this life? What do you think is your unique purpose?

TAKE STOCK OF YOUR GROWTH

When you shift your perspective to see your authentic, unique self, instead of seeing yourself in terms of where you stand in the world, you will begin to see your remarkable gifts that you had yet to discover. You will begin to look at yourself without judgment and see new ways to appreciate and love yourself for the special qualities you have.

As human beings, we often get discouraged and feel as if we're making little headway in life. When you feel that way, focus on your growth—the ways you have bettered yourself since you were born. Focusing on how you have grown will help you appreciate all the wisdom, abilities, and experiences you have gained over the years.

We often have growth potential in our weaker areas. So, for example, if we're confident in our physical strengths, we may want to develop experience and wisdom. Likewise, if intellect is where we excel, strengthening our willpower will often help our souls continue to develop. On the other hand, willpower that is too strong can lead to stubbornness and so needs to be balanced by intellect. It's often our strengths that bring success, but cultivating our weakest areas is pivotal for our lasting growth.

Whenever we lose one of our strengths, we end up gaining something else in its place that allows us to see things in a new light. For example, as we age, we may lose physical strength, but our years of experience reward us with wisdom that helps us make decisions quickly. Life is a state of constant change, so we may as well enjoy the ride. Find the joy and empowerment in transformation: commit to becoming better today than you were yesterday, and better tomorrow than you are today.

how much have you grown?

You've come a long way. How have you changed for the better?

What have you gained from your life experiences? Knowledge?
Abilities? Relationships?

....

....

....

....

....

....

....

....

....

....

....

....

....

....

....

....

....

....

....

....

....

In what ways have you grown?

Where do you feel stuck? How would you like to grow?

For everything we lose, we gain something new. For every loss you've experienced, note what you've gained in return.

LOSS		GAIN

hardships & failures

the tools for spiritual growth

One of the greatest secrets to happiness is knowing that you are the author of your life. We are all empowered with the ability to choose our own destiny, and we alone are responsible for the precious process of learning from our choices.

CALM IN THE FACE OF ADVERSITY

We all dream of reaching our goals and living without difficulties, but in reality, life can sometimes be so difficult that we end up feeling alone and helpless. Adversity is a part of life, and unfavorable winds sometimes blow. We face setbacks in school, in our careers, and in our relationships that we would avoid if we could. But as difficult as these setbacks may be, they are there because we have put them there. We ourselves have planned our lives so that our days are filled with challenges.

Before we were born, we knew how each experience would mold our character. We knew that each challenge in our path would help us to reflect deeply on ourselves, understand those around us, and, most importantly, see the world in a new light.

Misfortunes occur not to make us suffer but to enlighten our souls. As we reflect on our misfortunes, we may discover how much support we have received from others and how many of our achievements were possible because of their help. When these feelings of connection and love fill us, we become one with the power of the universe.

Calmly accepting our challenges is what saves us in the truest sense. When we fall into a pool drowning, stillness is how we save our lives. If we flail our arms and legs, we end up swallowing too much water, exhausting ourselves, and becoming more panicked. But when we stop moving, we naturally float to the surface. We can resolve our life difficulties with the same approach. If we sit still and quietly witness what's happening to us, we can resolve our problems with less energy, with less fear and emotional havoc, and without sinking. By calmly accepting our challenges as precious gifts for our spiritual growth, we become one with the will of the universe and see the helping hand it is extending.

We all have inherent abilities and talents, but these alone don't help us grow. It is the challenges we overcome that make our souls expand and shine. It is our strength, honesty, humility, and strong faith in our divine nature despite adversity that enhance the brilliance of our souls.

Adversity is painful. The key is not to put ourselves down or allow negative thinking to take over for too long. It is important to keep making an earnest effort to break through hardships. And even if we don't reach success, fate always has another door ready for us. Some situations will become clear within our lifetime, while others are hidden until we leave this earth. But the effort we put into conquering adversity is never futile.

TRY THIS OUT
ON THE NEXT PAGE

becoming one with the will of the universe

1   *Sit in a comfortable position with your palms upward on your knees in an area where you feel comfortable and are free from any distraction.*

2   *Close your eyes and slowly inhale and exhale. Inhale deeply through your nose and chest. Visualize the breath reaching your lower abdomen. Then exhale quietly and slowly through your mouth.*

3   *When you feel tranquil, close your eyes and visualize the great universe, with its numerous stars, in complete stillness. Feel the vastness and serenity that envelops you.*

4   *Let go of all your worries and negative emotions, and visualize them melting and being absorbed into the universe. Feel the great love of the universe.*

DOWNLOADABLE
MUSIC AVAILABLE AT
OKAWABOOKS.COM

angel tip

Sometimes we have great success that brings
excitement and joy, and other times failure that brings
great despair. Whatever we face, we can overcome by
humbly accepting it, learning from it,
and finding meaning in it.

When you're feeling lost in life, recite this to yourself:

"I am living my best life, the one that will
allow my unique gifts and my soul to develop
to the fullest, in accordance with the will of
the universe."

FAILURE:
YOUR SPRINGBOARD TO SUCCESS

The greater part of our life's learning comes not from success, but from failure. In truth, some of the richest seeds of creativity and progress are hidden within mistakes and failures. And most successes come on the heels of disappointment. In moments of failure, we must remind ourselves that our disappointments allow us to eliminate what wasn't working. We then reduce our chances of repeating the same disappointment and increase our odds for success the next go-around.

Every experience that falls short of success is a valuable opportunity for learning, self-reflection, and improvement. We discover why we weren't able to succeed and what were lacking—ability, expertise, the right timing, or particular circumstances—so

we can move onto conquering the next challenge. To achieve what we want in life, it's crucial to find these seeds of success within each mistake.

Those who have had the greatest successes are also often the most experienced in hardship, adversity, setback, and low self-esteem. Typically, the higher our ideals and aspirations, the more adversities we're faced with and the more mistakes we seem to make. What's crucial is how we rebound. The secret is repeatedly asking, "What is the lesson?" and then applying what we find to our next attempts.

Being highly capable tends to make us race hurriedly towards our goals. When we do that, we risk losing sight of other people's feelings, ignoring the deeper part of our hearts (our true self), and pushing ourselves too hard. The mistakes we make in pursuit of high goals are important opportunities for us to recharge, search our souls, and cultivate love and understanding for others.

There's a way to turn every mistake into a springboard that launches us toward our next positive step. This is true for not only our own mistakes, but also those of the people we meet throughout our lives. We can grow by learning from the successes and mistakes of those around us. By making a thorough study of others' personalities, how and why they fail, and what causes their errors, we gain a limitless source of learning and food for self-reflection. Failure is, very simply, some of our most potent fuel for facing our next challenge.

Often, we are simply unaware of the mistakes we've made. When everything is going well, we become blind to the potential cause of the next failure. But once you fail,

hindsight shows you clearly that the root of failure was seeded as many as five or ten years before, when all seemed to be going well. Failures and mistakes often expose our faults and weaknesses, but becoming aware of our shortcomings lets us move on to the next level of self-growth.

Life is a journey toward expansion of the self. A transformed self-awareness—a change in the way we see ourselves—is evidence that our souls have grown. To gain a higher perspective (or enlightenment), we are born into this world and go through various experiences, hardships, and difficulties. Every outcome offers a new door that opens up new possibilities. Even if a particular path doesn't open for us, we can reflect on why we didn't succeed and learn from what we discover. This learning then prepares us for the next step.

TRY THIS OUT
ON THE NEXT PAGE

learning from hardships and failures

What hardships or trials have you faced?

....
....
....
....
....
....
....
....
....

What are your greatest or most important failures?

....
....
....
....
....
....
....
....
....

What did your hardships, trials, and failures teach you? Why do you think they were necessary for your spiritual growth?

happy truth

No one in this world has ever failed in a true sense.
We're all born with the purpose of refining our souls by
going through various experiences, so there is no such
thing as absolute failure. We all play a temporary role
in this world, and everything we experience serves as a
lesson and as spiritual nourishment. When we see life
from this perspective, we're able to access our true
self—the part of us that knows our truth and never
feels discouraged or lost.

HARDSHIPS:
YOUR MISSION IN DISGUISE

Prayer is extremely important, but that doesn't mean that we should rely solely on divine intervention to help us solve our problems. It's only natural to pray when times are challenging and we're at our wits end. In fact, prayer is an essential part of practicing mindfulness and attaining spiritual peace and enlightenment. But to support our intentions and prayers, we need to do all that we can for ourselves. Exploring what positive steps we can take in our present situation allows us to stay in the present and avoid thoughts like "If I had only…" or "If that hadn't happened…." Focusing on our potential in the present reminds us that even in times of adversity, there's always some positive action we can take.

In times of difficulty, we empower ourselves by continually asking what we can do for the sake of others—family, school, friends, community, and society. The contributions we make to others, one by one, as we move forward with our lives allow our souls to truly grow.

All of us—nurses, doctors, patients, teachers, students, grocers, fishers, mechanics, government officials, construction workers, sisters, brothers, parents, and grandparents—have the mission to spread light in the world. And we can fulfill our purpose no matter what challenges we find ourselves in—even if we are confined to a hospital bed, have lost our job, or have been deserted by our own family. The environments surrounding us are all part of our individual lessons to help us fulfill our mission of light. If these lessons are too easy, we can be assured that more challenging ones will come. And when they seem unbearably difficult, they will gradually ease. The more each of us becomes aware of our own power to fulfill our purpose, the more we can increase love and light in this world.

TRY THIS OUT
ON THE NEXT PAGE

understanding your circumstances

The circumstances you find yourself in are merely lessons you need. What do they tell you about your life's purpose?

....
....
....
....
....
....
....
....

Are you facing any obstacles right now? Do you feel powerless to change things? Ask your inner angel what you can do in the circumstances you find yourself in now.

....
....
....
....
....
....
....
....

What contributions can you make to your family, school, company, community, or humankind?

....
....
....
....
....
....
....
....
....
....
....
....
....
....
....
....
....
....
....
....
....
....
....

mini-inspiration
a spiritual message from Hellen Keller

"You may be suffering from disabilities, misfortunes, or unhappiness. But they are part of the promise you made with God before coming to this world. You vowed that you would do your best to rise above any difficulties in this life, no matter how hard they are.

"We all consult with our angels as to what kind of life we choose to lead before we are born into this world. Those who are in adverse or disadvantageous circumstances now made promises that they would overcome the trials and tribulations that they face during the course of their lives.

"I dare say that those who are in adverse circumstances are the chosen ones. God expects them to overcome the adversity so that they will become a great encouragement to others. So do not lament your own misfortunes. You were born into this world to shine your divine glory.

"It is you, not anyone else, who chose your life. You chose your own fate, so embrace it."

EXCERPTED FROM RYUHO OKAWA
SPIRITUAL MESSAGE COLLECTION VOL. 14

your life mission.
your purpose.

1   Sit in a comfortable position with your palms upward on your knees in an area where you feel comfortable and free from any distraction.

2   Inhale and exhale slowly. Inhale deeply through the nose and chest. Visualize the breath reaching the lower abdomen. Then exhale quietly and slowly through the mouth. As you breathe, visualize the fresh blood and oxygen circulating throughout your entire body—your head, neck, shoulders, hips, etc. This will harmonize the vibrations in your mind and body.

3   Imagine that you are preparing to be born into this world. What do the issues you're facing now tell you about your mission in life and the spiritual promises you made in heaven?

DOWNLOADABLE
MUSIC AVAILABLE AT
OKAWABOOKS.COM

a spiritual promise
to yourself

In the "Your Life Mission. Your Purpose." exercise, what discoveries did you make about your mission in life and the promises you made before you were born?

....
....
....
....
....
....
....
....
....
....
....
....
....
....
....
....
....
....
....
....
....

gratitude

the gateway to happiness

Being happy with what we have is a
secret to the greatest happiness.
To be content is to love our lives,
embrace them for what they
are, and accept that we all have
unique lives of our own. We have
been blessed with so much to be
thankful for, including each of the
days of our lives.

DISCOVERING YOUR BLESSINGS

We've all experienced anxiety and faced situations that are so challenging that we've wished we could give up and run away. As simple as it may sound, a daily gratitude practice is a powerful tool for shifting your thinking in times like these. It can boost your mood even when you're in a negative place and feel that you have little to be grateful for—for example, when you're facing difficult circumstances or physical strain.

A gratitude statement can begin with something as basic as "I'm alive today," "Regardless of its hardships and troubles, today is a gift," "Our planet is still here," "The sun is shining," "I made it through yesterday," or "Tomorrow will be a new day."

Practicing gratitude really begins with going back to the very beginning of our lives and remembering how we originally started: as newborn babies with nothing of our own. Life itself was a great gift. Whether our family was wealthy or poor didn't matter to us then. We were just a little life with a tiny body weighing about seven pounds, quietly preparing for what lay ahead. You began as a baby with little to distinguish you from other babies. You may have been slightly lighter or heavier than others, but there was nothing about you that could have determined the outcome of your life. Right now, if you lined up hundreds of babies in front of you, you would not be able to tell what kind of life each baby will lead. But since that point in your life, you've grown up and have been living your own unique life with your own unique thoughts and actions.

We were given so much throughout childhood—clothes, food, a home, an allowance, an education, teachers, friends, school supplies, televisions, radios, stereos, and, above all, hope for a bright future. These were all gifts we were blessed with. In spite of all these gifts, many of us formed a negative self-image and developed a habit of focusing on the minuses in life. We compared ourselves with others in school, at home, and at work. There were good times when we were recognized for our contributions and other times when we were not. During these low points, it was easy to focus on criticisms and hurt and to forget about the love, kindness, and positive words we had received. A gratitude practice helps shift us away from this kind of thinking and refocus on life's pluses.

When we look back on our lives from the very beginning, we see that we've been blessed with wonderful friends and family who have helped us accomplish much more than we might have realized. We've all received the help, love, and support of many people, both directly and indirectly. We are who we are today because of the love of a great many people.

Gratitude practices awaken us to the value of being happy with our blessings. Gradually, our perspective on life changes, and we open our eyes to the abundance of love we have already received. Gratitude is a power that illuminates the wonderful blessings that used to be hidden from our vision until they become clear and bright.

TRY THIS OUT
ON THE NEXT PAGE

gratitude practice

Both directly and indirectly, you have received the help and love of many people.

Every day, identify ten things you're blessed with and write them down in a list, name them out loud, or simply think them to yourself.

1 ....

2 ....

3 ....

4 ....

5 ....

6 ....

7 ....

8 ....

9 ....

10 ....

What help, love, support, or care have you received from others today or at some other time in your life?

....

....

....

....

....

....

....

....

....

If you haven't been practicing, or if you're feeling extremely down, you might find it difficult to think of things to be grateful for. But after you've been practicing a while, you'll easily think of a limitless number of things to be grateful for. Until then, here's a list of things you can repeat to yourself when you come up empty.

* *I started with nothing at birth, and I'm still here.*

* *I'm grateful for all the love my parents gave me.*

* *I'm grateful for my education.*

* *I'm grateful for my friends.*

* *I'm grateful that I made it through yesterday.*

YOUR BALANCE SHEET OF LOVE

If you could remember all the help, support, and love you've received in your lifetime, it would be an endless list. What about when you reflect on the selfless kindness you've extended to others? Create a balance sheet of love by listing the love you've received on the left and the love you've given on the right. The list of love you have received will most likely be much longer than the list of love you have given. Now, when you want to be inspired by gratitude, all you have to do is refer to your balance sheet.

As you create your balance sheet, you'll notice right away how much you've been given ever since you were born. Your parents fed you milk, changed your diapers, cradled you when you cried, and put you to sleep. They took care of

you when you acted selfishly or cried at night as a baby. Then in kindergarten and throughout your childhood, your parents and teachers took good care of you when you hurt yourself, got sick, or got into trouble. On the other hand, you will probably have a hard time thinking of things to write in the "Love You Gave" column from when you were a baby. You may end up thinking of even more kinds of care you received, like being bathed every day.

Even at age one, two, or three, there is not much we can write in the "Love You Gave" column. The best we can do is say that we made our parents happy—for example, when we were born without complications, when we learned to stand up by ourselves, when we started talking, or just by being adorable. You may be able to think of a few things to write down in this column from your elementary school years, such as times when you were nice to your parents. And you may have a handful of memories of giving love during middle school and high school, but probably not much more.

Until we become Independent at around age twenty, most of us lead very self-absorbed lives, taking as much support and love as possible from those around us in preparation for adulthood. Even as college students, we continue to concentrate on self-growth. This is not a bad thing—after all, children need to be nurtured to grow up healthy and happy. Our opportunities to repay the debt we owe begin when we reach adulthood and become members of society.

The purpose of this exercise is not to make you feel horrible—it's to help you feel gratitude. When you're strug-gling with a strong sense of unhappiness, thinking about how much love you've given and comparing that with how much love you've received can help you once again feel grateful for your blessings.

As you do this exercise, you might discover that even during times when you were complaining, criticizing others, and feeling discontented and dissatisfied, you were still receiving an abundance of love all the while. When we're miserable, it's easy to think thoughts like "Why didn't he do that for me?" and "This went wrong," and "That went wrong." We might feel like criticizing someone every time we have the chance. But when we shift to focusing on the love we've received, we feel better and better about ourselves and our lives.

TRY THIS OUT
ON THE NEXT PAGE

adding up love

Make a balance sheet, putting "love you received" as a heading on one side and "love you gave" on the other.

LOVE YOU RECEIVED   **LOVE YOU GAVE**

UP TO KINDERGARTEN

ELEMENTARY SCHOOL

MIDDLE SCHOOL

HIGH SCHOOL

COLLEGE

20S TO 30S

30S AND ON

GIVING LOVE
CAN CHANGE YOUR LIFE

Every day, we can choose to give gratefully to everyone and repay the love we have been given throughout our lives. We can approach every day as a kind of experiment: how much more love can we give than take?

The love we give is different from the love we take. Love that gives is a selfless manifestation of the wish to give. In contrast, love that takes is an attachment—a self-serving desire for self-protection and control. This type of love is an attempt to bind others and deprive them of their freedom, and it is not a real or lasting love. A generous, selfless, giving love may inspire you to give money and gifts to someone you love. But if your aim is actually to bind the other person to you, then no matter how much money

or how many gifts you give, you are taking from them. This is why love vanishes when we expect something in return for what we provide.

True love is selfless. It does not expect anything in return. True love sets people free. It helps others grow and develop fully because it trusts in their goodness. True love is also so unconditional: lovers keep on giving and sharing even when they won't be able to enjoy the reward of seeing their loved ones blossom. True love is like the sun: it neither rests nor ever stops giving its light and warmth.

Love that gives can also be called compassion; it's the core of human nature and the will of God. It treats everyone equally and gives without discrimination. The essence of love is to find the light in everyone and everything and to appreciate and praise it. We can cherish and find wonder in other beings, a simple flower, or even a tiny insect. Love helps us find the divine nature that radiates in us and in every person we meet. This gives love its power to heal the wounds of hurt and inferiority. When we were born, none of us felt ashamed or compared ourselves with others. But as we grew older, many of us developed feelings of inferiority because we believed that we were unloved. As we look around now, we can see other people suffering from feelings of inferiority, and we come to understand how important it is to give love. The more pain our own feelings of inferiority cause us, the more we understand that the world needs our love. Being a giver of love can help us get rid of our feelings of inferiority.

When we give love, we must give it continually, without expecting anything in return, because that is love's true nature. To love is to keep on sowing seeds and planting bulbs even if you do not get to see them when they bloom.

It is easy to say that it's important to treat others with compassion, but it's more challenging to practice compassion on a daily basis. What does it mean to extend compassion and love to others? That's something that we all must try to discover for ourselves. We must take the path of daily reflection on the kindness, compassion, and love we extend and receive. Sharing love, kindness, and compassion with others is a life-changing spiritual lesson that we can begin practicing right away.

As soon as you decide to be compassionate, many people may come to you to offer their help. This may sound mysterious, but by a spiritual principle, help comes to us when we begin to help others; the love we give away actually comes back to us in the end.

When we do something purely for the sake of others, a halo appears above our heads the minute the thought enters our mind and is put into action. This halo is invisible to the eyes of those on earth, but it comes from heaven as light. You can sense this halo by noticing that your body starts to feel warm whenever you do something out of a pure intention to make others happy. Even in the middle of winter, both the givers and the receivers of pure love will feel filled with warmth. So when your thoughts are full of love for others, you are actually on the receiving end of it, too.

TRY THIS OUT
ON THE NEXT PAGE

love and compassion. giving and getting.

1   *What can you do out of selfless love to help another grow?*

....

....

....

....

....

....

....

....

....

2   *Are there people in your life that you attempt to change or control?*

....

....

....

....

....

....

....

....

3   How have you given and shared love unconditionally?

....

....

....

....

....

....

....

....

....

....

4   To whom and how can you extend more kindness or
    compassion?

....

....

....

....

....

....

....

....

....

....

LIVING A LIFE OF KINDNESS

Even though it may be a bit frightening, imagining how we'd feel if we had to leave this world today can help us find out how we want to practice being loving. It's a fact that each of us eventually returns to the other world. It will feel as if we are flying above the Earth and becoming a star in the sky. As you fly thousands of feet up into the sky, the Earth will become a tiny ball. Memories of your childhood playground, your home, and your friends will become ever so distant and tiny. The woods, the rivers, the mountains, and all that was once familiar will become hazy.

When this moment arrives, you might wish you had given more kindness, spoken more compassionately, and been more loving to everyone who was dear to you. Life on earth is evanescent, like the fragments of our memories of fairy tales we read long ago, classroom trips, or happy days at school. So, since you will be leaving this world eventually, why not fill it with warm and sweet memories, and why not treat others with kindness, the way you love to be treated? The happiest moments in life are those when we received the simple gift of kindness.

TRY THIS OUT
ON THE NEXT PAGE

kindness practice

The following are questions you can ask yourself every day to review your actions and words and consider how to offer more compassion to others:

Were there any conversations, interactions, or conflicts in which you could have found kinder words? Write down what you said and how you could rephrase it to be more compassionate.

What you said:

....
....
....
....
....
....
....

How you would rephrase it:

....
....
....
....
....
....
....

Think about the small actions that you took in the course of your day. Which of them could you have put more kindness and thoughtfulness into? Write what happened and then how you'd like to react in the future in a similar situation.

What happened:

....
....
....
....
....
....
....
....

How you'd react in the future:

....
....
....
....
....
....
....
....
....
....

PUTTING YOUR LOVE INTO ACTION

Love is not just an abstract feeling; love is also action. At the end of every day, you can check whether you were loving by reflecting on whether you were as kind and helpful as you could be. Sometimes, the challenges of daily life can get the best of us, and we can spend whole days, weeks, or more preoccupied with our own lives. So now let's shift our focus away from ourselves, our pride, our self-admiration, and our self-preservation and take a moment to reflect on what we were able to do for others today, this week, this month, and this year.

TRY THIS OUT
ON THE NEXT PAGE

love in action

Make answering these questions a daily practice for the next seven days as part of setting an intention for further spiritual development.

How have you put love and kindness into action? How might you have been more kind? Is there anything you could have done more thoughtfully or respectfully?

DAY 1

DATE:

....
....
....
....
....
....
....
....
....
....
....
....
....
....

DAY 2

DATE:

....
....
....
....
....
....
....
....
....

DAY 3

DATE:

....
....
....
....
....
....
....
....
....

DAY 4

DATE:

....

....

....

....

....

....

....

....

DAY 5

DATE:

....

....

....

....

....

....

....

....

....

DAY 6

DATE:

....
....
....
....
....
....
....
....

DAY 7

DATE:

....
....
....
....
....
....
....
....
....

In the coming days and weeks, what small kindnesses can you extend to loved ones, strangers, colleagues, and neighbors?

forgiveness

cultivating compassion within

While we all have divine nature within us, we're still imperfect. And that's how we're meant to be. We're all here to learn from our various experiences in this world and grow our souls. Remembering this can help us tolerate imperfections and forgive mistakes—both our own and others'.

ACCEPTING
IMPERFECTION

There are more than seven billion people in the world today, and not one lives a perfect life. Everyone has flaws and regrets. We're all imperfect. We all make mistakes and experience failure at some point in life. But these experiences lead to discoveries and spiritual growth. Understanding this helps us cultivate compassion toward others who are going through the same process as they try to open up a new path in life.

We often suffer because we want to live a perfect life, but we know we can't avoid failure and errors as long as we live in this world. If you contemplate your mistakes and find that you are blaming yourself for your imperfections, remind yourself to live a better life, but not a perfect one. Instead of seeking 100 percent perfection in your life, why not try for 70 percent? When we are content with 70 percent, we're better able to accept what we have, where we are in our lives, and even ourselves for who we really are. We will always have regrets, but we can practice being less judgmental of ourselves and our lives by focusing on the positive 70 percent. In this way, the positive always outweighs the negative.

Each of us has the creative power to transform freely according to our own will. We have the power to become whatever type of consciousness we wish to be and to choose our actions as well. Conflict often comes when we rely on our own standards to criticize, condemn, or judge others as they act according to their own will.

By focusing on the brilliant divine nature inside each of us, we realize how precious and wonderful we all can become.

TRY THIS OUT
ON THE NEXT PAGE

finding your 70 percent

What would it mean for you to live a 70 percent positive life?

....

....

....

....

....

....

....

What makes you happy to be the way you are?

I am happy with myself when/because ....

....

....

....

....

....

....

....

....

....

....

....

....

THE COURAGE TO FORGIVE YOURSELF

We all wish to overcome the challenges we face in life, but sometimes we find ourselves fighting a losing battle and enduring loss. When we find ourselves failing despite all our best efforts and wisdom, what we need above all is the courage to forgive ourselves. We may begin to fall into negative thinking and self-blame, but when we make a practice of focusing on the positive—knowing we did our best—we can stop self-depreciating thoughts and find the cour-age to begin again. We can learn from what went wrong and take responsibility for what we can do better next time. We can let go and stop suffering.

It takes courage to forgive ourselves for our failures. But with each failure, we gain the experience and wisdom that we need for our spiritual growth—and that growth is what makes our lives in this world meaningful.

TRY THIS OUT
ON THE NEXT PAGE

forgiving yourself

If your mind lingers on regrets, write down the one that bothers you most.

....
....
....
....

What lessons did you learn from this experience?

....
....
....
....
....
....
....
....
....
....
....
....
....
....
....
....

You've done your best, and you've suffered long enough. To help you find the courage to forgive yourself, write yourself a letter of forgiveness.

Dear me,

....

....

....

....

....

....

....

....

....

....

....

....

....

....

....

....

....

....

....

....

....

....

THE SPIRITUAL POWER
OF FORGIVENESS

Forgiveness is not only an earthly power, but also a spiritual power: it is the power of love. Forgiveness is not an abstract concept; it is an indispensable component of happiness. Only when we can forgive one another will we all find happiness in this world.

We can overcome negative emotions and find peace of mind by accepting the people who have disappointed us and letting go of our regrets about the past. A simple practice of letting go offers many blessings: we sleep better at night; we feel refreshed and lighter, as though a burden has been lifted; and we sense the compassion that others have extended to us.

As imperfect beings, we sometimes find ourselves slipping into negative thoughts and holding on to feelings of anger or resentment. It's not always easy to let go of these feelings, but we get better at it with practice. One of the most critical steps is to try to see things from the other person's perspective. When we do this, we sometimes uncover circumstances and beliefs that help us understand the other person and help us shift from anger to compassion. When we stand in other people's shoes and speak to ourselves from their perspective, it changes how we think about speaking to them and helps us cultivate compassion and forgiveness. And this, in turn, frees us.

Nothing in this world goes exactly the way we want it to, so we sometimes have to accept things as they are, especially when it comes to other people. Even in the most extreme cases, when forgiveness is a tremendous challenge, it's necessary for our own health and peace of mind. Forgiveness, in the end, is a gift to ourselves much more than to others. Sustained subconscious negativity can eventually make us sick, but forgiveness has healing power. Forgiveness is a spiritual state: by practicing it, we cultivate a deep love that can cure both others and ourselves. Forgiveness may not always come naturally, but by consciously reminding ourselves of its power, we can free ourselves from resentment and find peace of mind.

TRY THIS OUT
ON THE NEXT PAGE

save the date to save yourself

You may find that, despite all your efforts, you're still having trouble forgiving yourself or other people. In that case, set a time limit for your suffering. Decide when you will let go of the bitter feeling lingering inside you. It could be by the end of today, by the end of the week, or by the end of the month. Write it on your calendar, planner, a sticky note, or anywhere you're sure to see it. Treat it as an actual event that's taking place at a specific time, and make sure you take action on it.

I will let go of...
....
....
....
....
....
....
....
....
....
....
....
....

BY DATE/TIME: ....

UNDERSTANDING:
THE ROOT OF FORGIVENESS

There are dimensions of other people that we never see. Remembering this can help us maintain an open, compassionate, nonjudgmental mind. Just as we don't always feel completely understood, we misunderstand others when we see them only from our own limited perspective. When we take our assumptions for granted, we easily create unnecessary misunderstandings and resentments. When we indulge the feeling that we know better than other people, we risk developing unforgiving heart. To develop a tolerant, forgiving heart, we must let go of our assumptions and really get to know one another. We must work to understand where others are coming from, what they've been through, and how they feel.

We can harmonize our relationships with others by seeing them as unique masterpieces of God. Every famous painting elicits an entire spectrum of perspectives and opinions. Some love what others can't stand. But it's this difference in how each painting expresses beauty and ideas that makes a painting valuable. Accepting others' perspectives is about developing compassion, tolerance, appreciation, and forgiveness.

relationship harmony

If a difficult relationship is troubling you, you can find peace of mind by contemplating how you might resolve it in a way you hadn't considered before.

1   *Sit in a comfortable position in your sanctuary, and gently close your eyes. Practice some meditative breathing to prepare for the visualization.*

2   *Look within. Do you find yourself upset by negative feelings about another person? Is there anyone from your past or present life that you associate with difficult experiences, hardships, sorrow, or pain?*

3   *Imagine this person sitting in front of you. Visualize yourself saying, "I'd really like to understand you better. Can you help me?" With an open, calm mind, listen to what he or she says in reply.*

4   *Next, consider, what you don't know about this person that could change how you feel.*

5   *Imagine that your relationship with this person has improved and you are now on good terms. What positive dialogue with this person can you visualize taking place?*

6   *Can you imagine shaking hands or hugging after your conversation?*

DOWNLOADABLE
MUSIC AVAILABLE AT
OKAWABOOKS.COM

turning conflict into compassion

After you have finished the "Relationship Harmony" exercise, think about your conflict with this person. How do you feel about it now?

....
....
....
....
....
....
....
....
....

What can you do now to improve your relationship with him or her?

....
....
....
....
....
....
....
....
....

How might your experience with this person be an opportunity to cultivate understanding and a compassionate heart?

HAPPINESS IN THE NOW

We can't change what happened in the past, but we can change our future. We have the power to manifest what we want in our lives. At the same time, when we find happiness in the present, we see our past in a different and more positive light.

When we are happy, we recognize that everyone we've ever met was meant to move us toward happiness. Even those who hurt or wronged us become an integral part of our path of happiness. Each serves as a whetstone to refine our soul. Each one helped us become who we are today.

All of us have both the right and the responsibility to be happy. Taking responsibility for our happiness allows us to cultivate compassion and acknowledge one another. It's by understanding others' perspectives and lifestyles that we come to see their strengths and brilliance. When we truly honor our own and everyone else's right to and responsibility for happiness, we will be able to create the kind of world we'd all like to see.

TRY THIS OUT
ON THE NEXT PAGE

your right and responsibility to be happy

What makes you happy now? Who has contributed to your happiness?

....
....
....
....
....
....
....

What does it mean for you to take responsibility for your own happiness?

....
....
....
....
....
....
....
....
....
....

What can you do to honor other people's right to happiness?

....
....
....
....
....
....
....
....
....
....

How would you like to contribute to making this world a happier place?

....
....
....
....
....
....
....
....
....
....

a joyful life

surrounding yourself with the positive

Lightheartedness is the starting point of happiness. Think simply and positively, be carefree and hopeful, and live joyfully. This practice will awaken you to the power of faith and the divine nature within you.

A HEART FILLED WITH LIGHT

What would life be like if we lived without distress, doubts, and sadness? If fewer things felt like problems, we would feel carefree and live more simply and positively. Every day would feel like basking in joy. We would be relaxed and fulfilled as we enjoyed the beauty of life.

When we're dedicated to living joyfully, everything seems simpler, and anger and heartache leave our lives almost completely. We're overcome with a new sense of ease when we learn we have the power to just let go—the power to choose to let things just roll off our backs, like a little kid who forgets all the worries of the day after a night's sleep.

It only takes a small amount of effort to live this way. When we catch thoughts, events, and others' comments replaying in our head, we can choose to let go of the ones that don't serve us.

Shifting your thinking this way changes your experiences. Complex ideas no longer pile up in your mind, and heavy burdens are replaced with a sense of freedom. The key is to feel the lightness. It's like removing winter clothes to dress in a spring outfit. It's that simple. We tend to "put on" different kinds of heavy thoughts unconsciously. But if we choose not to, we can lighten our load.

flowing stream visualization

Living a lighthearted life means letting your mind flow like a stream so that sunlight twinkles off the surface where there once was darkness. Under warm sunlight, let your heart flow without obstruction.

1   *Sit in a comfortable position in your sanctuary. Gently close your eyes. Inhale and exhale slowly and deeply until you feel calm.*

2   *Imagine a shallow stream less than a foot deep. It's moving slowly and bathed in gentle spring sunlight. The riverbed sparkles with the gold tones and gentle patterns of sunlight filtering down from the surface. Imagine the shimmering sand below the water.*

3   *Hear the peaceful murmur of the water. What else do you hear?*

4   *Smell the air. What do you smell?*

5   *Feel the warmth of the sun. How do you feel? What thoughts or feelings come up?*

DOWNLOADABLE
MUSIC AVAILABLE AT
OKAWABOOKS.COM

CREATING
MOMENTS OF JOY

Finding joy in the smallest things will surround you with an air of positiveness. Look for things that can uplift you or give you a boost. Try something simple and easy but new and different—for example, eating out at the exquisite restaurant you've been wanting to try or wearing the shoes or dress that you fell in love with but have never had a chance to wear. Focusing on the little things that give you joy will create lasting, uplifting change in your life. It's often the simplest things that have the power to open us to a new path in life.

simple pleasures

1   *Sit in a comfortable position with your palms upward on your knees in an area where you feel comfortable and are free from any distraction.*

2   *Close your eyes. Inhale deeply through your nose and chest. Visualize the breath reaching your lower abdomen. Then slowly and quietly exhale through your mouth.*

3   *When you feel tranquil, review the different moments of your day, and look for the joy in each of them. What did you do when you got up this morning? Did you enjoy your breakfast? Did you meet people you could say hello to?*

4   *Did you have a fulfilling day at work? Did you enjoy a quiet day at home? Feel the joy in even the smallest things, such as being able to breathe or having had a good night's sleep.*

DOWNLOADABLE
MUSIC AVAILABLE AT
OKAWABOOKS.COM

finding one good thing every day

Living joyfully starts with discovering something good in your life every day. Many people live by the motto, "Do one good turn every day." But even if you couldn't do a good turn, simply *finding* one good thing in your life every day will be a giant step forward on the path to happiness.

What is one good thing that happened today? How did it make your life more joyful?

....

....

....

....

....

Repeat this practice for seven days, and record the joy you find.

DAY 1

DATE:

....

....

....

....

....

DAY 2

DATE:

....
....
....
....
....

DAY 3

DATE:

....
....
....
....
....

DAY 4

DATE:

....
....
....
....
....

DAY 5

DATE:

....
....
....
....
....

DAY 6

DATE:

....
....
....
....
....

DAY 7

DATE:

....
....
....
....
....

GIVE THE GIFT
OF A SMILE

A smile is one of the simplest gifts of compassion. It's a moment of connection, a moment when we share joy and warmth. Smiling makes us feel better, so it's no surprise that it also makes us look better and attracts more happiness to us. When we smile, we emit soft, warm vibrations and release tension in the body, which opens us up so we can receive more heavenly light.

A smile is a gift we can share freely with strangers and loved ones. The more we share our smile with others, the more joy we bring them. Smiling can be a practice: our smile is something we have the power to create. We have no idea what hardships and sorrow those around us are experiencing—all we can see is that they've failed to share their smile. Our own challeng-

ing times are ideal opportunities to shift from a negative to a positive outlook by sharing the compassion of our smile. And when we smile, we are rewarded too—with the uplifting and joyous feelings that smiling brings.

Practicing sharing our smile doesn't mean faking or masking our true feelings—it means finding joy and beauty in what's around us. Making the effort to share a smile with others immediately empowers us to lift their spirits—and to increase our own happiness, in turn.

One of the secrets to living in joy is to smile often. A smile is truly an offering of connection and compassion—one we can easily share with everyone around us. And the more we share this gift, the better our world will become.

smile power

Sit in front of a mirror and smile. Try not to force it—make it as natural as possible. Find your best smiling face. How do you feel?

....

....

....

....

....

....

....

....

Find something compassionate and kind to say to the person in the mirror. ("You're beautiful," "I love you," etc.) Say it like you mean it. This self-kindness will induce your natural smile. What did you say to make yourself smile?

....

....

....

....

....

....

....

....

....

List the places and people with whom you could be sharing more smiles. Your coffeehouse? Work? Grocery store? School? List some places or people with whom you've been missing the opportunity to look others in the eye and smile.

PEOPLE	PLACES

THINK
POSITIVE

The secret to success and happiness is planting the right seeds in our minds and helping those seeds grow. By planting the right seeds, we give our lives direction— we point ourselves toward our dreams, goals, and aspirations. Planting seeds is a way of telling ourselves where our destination lies and how to get there without drifting or losing our way. The secret is simple—when we're filled with positive thoughts, good things and people appear around us. We face the exciting challenge of using our power to think positively to create a wonderful life. The trick is to stay aware of the thoughts that go through our minds throughout the day. As simple as it sounds, this practice helps us mindfully shift from the negative to the positive. It is as easy as replacing any negative thought with anything about it that's positive.

What negative thoughts seem to come to your mind most often? If we want to break the habit of lingering on or constantly returning to pessimistic, negative, or judgmental thoughts, we need to regularly practice discarding what doesn't serve us. When you have a negative thought, try replacing it with a positive thought. If you're having difficulty at work and you can't stop thinking negatively about your job, shift your perspective: think about the joy you find at home or outside of work, and tell others about those joys. Focus on the list of things that bring you joy, no matter how small they are. Our ability to attract happiness is directly related to the time we spend in positive thought.

We all have positive thoughts, but we tend not to notice them. The more we can focus our energies on cultivating a positive outlook, the more our negative thoughts will be driven from our minds.

And the better we get at being positive, the more we'll notice good things happening around us. When we are filled with positive energy, there is little room in our lives for anything else.

TRY THIS OUT
ON THE NEXT PAGE

replacing negative thoughts with joy

List the negative thoughts that repeatedly recur in your mind. Becoming conscious of these thoughts will help you stop them as soon as they come to mind. Next, think about what positive thoughts you can replace these negative thoughts with.

NEGATIVE THOUGHT	REPLACED BY	POSITIVE THOUGHT
I had a terrible day at work.	→	I can enjoy a relaxing time at home.
	→	
	→	
	→	
	→	
	→	
	→	
	→	

Find seeds of happiness in your surroundings. Create a list of things that make you happy.

✱ ....
✱ ....
✱ ....
✱ ....
✱ ....
✱ ....
✱ ....
✱ ....
✱ ....
✱ ....
✱ ....
✱ ....
✱ ....
✱ ....
✱ ....
✱ ....
✱ ....
✱ ....
✱ ....
✱ ....

angel tip

Sometimes, negative thoughts seem to appear from
nowhere. But they can only linger if we have a shortage
of positive thoughts. Just as we turn on the lights to
drown out the darkness, we can practice "turning on"
positive thoughts so they can drown out whatever
negative thoughts arise.

USE POSITIVE WORDS

Words are an invisible energy with the power to boost or drain our daily mood. When we are in distress or despair, pessimistic words arise without our even realizing it. We can honor our true selves by refraining from speaking pessimistic or negative words that taint our hearts, and instead speaking about something that makes us happy. Choosing positive words is choosing love—for others and ourselves. Every time we speak, we're listening to what we're saying to ourselves and engraving into our minds the patterns of our words.

The words we speak also reach others' hearts, creating ripple effects of happiness or unhappiness. Because words change how we see ourselves and how we communicate with others, choosing positive and constructive words is one of the secrets to happiness.

Our joy increases when we share it with others. The more people you can share your joy with, the happier you will become. As your circle of happiness grows, your joy will become even more authentic.

TRY THIS OUT
ON THE NEXT PAGE

sharing the good things

When we share the good things in our lives, it not only makes us feel better, but also makes the people around us feel better.

Tell people you know about the good things that have happened in your life during the last seven days. Write down how you felt when you shared these good things with others.

I shared ....
....
....
....
....
....

with ....
....

and felt ....
....
....
....
....
....
....

Ask people you know about the good things that have happened to them. Then write down what they told you and how it made you feel.

They shared ....

....

....

....

....

....

....

....

with me, and I felt ....

....

....

....

....

....

....

....

....

....

....

....

....

REFLECTING YOUR HAPPINESS ONTO OTHERS

No one but you is responsible for manifesting your positive self-image. Often, the most unkind and judgmental thoughts we have are the ones we think about ourselves. When we find ourselves easily hurt by others' remarks, it's because our ego—our small, insecure self—has leaked our power to the other person so that their criticisms mean more to us than our own inner truth. We can choose whether to let such remarks hurt our hearts or to let them pass and find inner peace. Always remind yourself to have a bright, constructive image of yourself, and reflect that image in your action.

Even if you're filled with happiness, unhappy people can pour cold water on you and spoil it. You may encounter people who tease or criticize you, causing you distress and pain. But neither letting these people disturb your mind nor avoiding these people completely will lead you to happiness.

No matter what happens, we can make each event a seed of our happiness, a lesson that can contribute to our spiritual abundance and growth. Even if someone criticizes us for our shortcomings, we can still gain valuable lessons in how others experience us; we can learn to reflect on ourselves; and we can accept the criticism and then let it go. When we practice responding to life this way, we find gratitude for the lessons we learn from even uncomfortable experiences.

The key is to shift your focus from reducing the number of unhappy people in your life to increasing the number of happy people you know. This way, you will fill your life with people who understand, support, and encourage you. Hold deep in your heart an earnest and strong wish to create as many happy people as possible who will join you in expanding the virtuous circle of happiness.

happy truth

We human beings can't survive alone, but we thrive
in communities. If you have kept your happiness
all to yourself, it is like a single flower in a vase: it's
beautiful, but lonely. Helping others' flowers to bloom
not only will give you greater joy and happiness, but
also will make the world more beautiful, like a field
filled with flowers in full bloom.

BELIEVE.
THE FIRST STEP TO A BETTER TOMORROW.

Believing that tomorrow will be a better day is the simplest form of faith. Positive thoughts can manifest changes in our outlook and mood. In difficult times, we can set our own perspective by repeating an affirming thought stated as a fact—for example, "I'm in the process of making my life better" or "My life is getting better each day." Affirmations like these condition your mind to think positively, and this conditioning makes your life shine more brightly. Worrying that things may take a turn for the worse doesn't serve us in any way, and neither does focusing on negative thoughts that keep us stuck in the past. Remember: each experience, bad or good, taught us something that has allowed us to more fully enjoy the beauty of today.

Imagine an entire world filled with people practicing a belief that today is better than yesterday and that tomorrow will be even better. The energy and faces of everyone we came in contact with would change for the better. We could live in joy, find kindness in the eyes of others, and radiate happiness from within. It sounds simple, but having a positive outlook is truly one of the easiest, most powerful ways to change everything in our lives.

Our minds have the power to create what we think, so imprinting your mind with positive images can move your life in a positive direction. You can also influence others to think more positively. If you see someone in a bad mood, you could say, "Why not believe that today is better than yesterday and that tomorrow will be even better than today? It can't rain forever; the sun will shine some day. You may be feeling awful right now, but these negative emotions will eventually go away, and then you'll feel happy again. Everything will be better if you simply believe."

A happy person believes in a bright future and is convinced that life can only get better. It all really does get better when we believe. We can create a better future and even a better world when each one of us believes that we're improving every day.

PUSHING THE
FRONTIERS OF YOUR LIFE

When we wake up in the morning feeling refreshed and motivated, free of fear, and filled with positive energy, we're primed to share our gifts and energy with everyone around us. And in this small way, we boost the world's happiness.

There are no outside conditions for happiness. We don't need grades, degrees, or specific material items to make us happy. Happiness is truly "equal opportunity"— open to all. We can start living a fulfilled and meaningful life no matter where we stand in life. All we have to do is make up our minds to open a new path and go forward courageously. You and you alone can push the frontiers of your life.

Our physical lives will come to an end some day, but our souls continue on. What our future becomes depends on how we've lived our lives and what we've learned in this lifetime. The next several decades of your life in this world will determine what your next life will be like. Right now, you have the power to transform every day into a sparkling, golden day and open up a bright future for yourself, here and in the world beyond.

dreams & goals

keys to empowering your potential

With persistence, we have the power to achieve our dreams. You can create a happy future for yourself by continually thinking positively and by visualizing your true self manifested in the present.

VISUALIZE, THEN REALIZE YOUR IDEAL SELF

Over time, we become the person we think we are. We have infinite possibilities to manifest a happy life for ourselves by creating the self-image that we want. Our lives imitate and shape themselves into what we envision. If we make a regular practice of visualizing ourselves behaving bravely in situations where we might otherwise be meek, we'll see a change. If we often find ourselves thinking about something negative that happened in the past, such as a mistake we made, we may be allowing the past to hold us back from being positive in the present. We may be so afraid of making another mistake that our fear keeps happiness out of our reach. So for those of us who find ourselves thinking negatively, the best thing to do is use visualization to replace the mental image of our mistake with a vision of ourselves acting positively. We can design our lives and create ourselves as the constructive and happy people we want to be.

We can bring our dreams closer to reality by repeatedly picturing our deepest ideals and holding them in our minds. We often keep our deepest ideals unconscious, but when we repeatedly bring them into our conscious imagination, they actualize into our lives. Our power to persistently visualize who we want to be is a clue that we may have the gifts we need to actualize our vision. We are all born with unique abilities and dispositions that allow us to reach the goals we were born to achieve. If we didn't have the potential to reach our goals, we would find it difficult to keep visualizing them. Conversely, if we find it difficult to visualize some of our ideals, it may be a clue that those ideals are not right for us. The dreams we keep dreaming are the ones that create our goals and destination in life.

angel tip

It's impossible for the human mind to think of two different things simultaneously. If you notice negative thoughts cropping up so often that it's difficult to stop them, fill your mind with the constructive actions you plan to take and images of a happy, wonderful life. Allow these images to become your powerful shield against negative thinking.

SET GOALS. MAKE PLANS.
CREATE YOUR LIFE'S BLUEPRINT.

Our thoughts are the blueprint of our lives. They have tremendous physical power to affect our future. Even when we don't notice our thoughts, subconsciously they are always influencing our path. In this way, each of our thoughts is like a child that, once it is born, begins to exercise its creative power and takes on a life of its own. This is why it's so critical that we choose our thoughts carefully. Like blueprints, our thoughts should be designed thoughtfully and with clarity. A clear vision of our intentions attracts others who are interested in our dreams and able to support them. If we explain repeatedly to many people how our building will look, where we plan to build it, and what its purpose will be, those who are not interested will simply pass by, but those who are interested will find it fascinating. If your building is a factory for Persian carpets, an interior designer might be attracted to it and even offer help. She'll also share your idea with her friends, and they might also offer to pitch in. Setting clearly defined goals is a powerful act: it sets your own focus and captivates the imaginations of like-minded others, both of which increase the chances that your dream will take shape.

visualizing your dream

Our guardian angels know everything we are thinking about. So when we hold a possible future strongly in our imagination, it reaches them.

1   *Sit in a comfortable position with your palms facing down on your knees in an area where you feel comfortable and free from any distraction.*

2   *Inhale and exhale slowly. Inhale deeply through the nose and chest. Visualize the breath reaching the lower abdomen. Then exhale quietly and slowly through the mouth.*

3   *Visualize clear images of the dreams you want to achieve.*

4   *Put your hands in prayer, and ask your inner angel to help you realize them when the time's right.*

DOWNLOADABLE
MUSIC AVAILABLE AT
OKAWABOOKS.COM

design your life

Write your vision for the dreams and goals you want to achieve. Make it a clear picture that articulates what you want to accomplish with your time on this world.

TIPS

* *Make sure your vision aligns with your true self and honest intentions.*

* *Keep it clear and descriptive.*

* *Write it in the present tense, as if it's happening now. Believe that it's coming true, right now.*

What is your vision for the life you want in .... years?

I am .... years old.

I live in ....

I enjoy ....

I've become ....

I've experienced ....

I've achieved ....

I've contributed to ....

I aspire to ....

....

....

When you're finished, close your eyes and visualize what you wrote down happening right now, in the present.

Where do you see yourself in .... years?

spiritual

* ....
* ....
* ....
* ....
* ....
* ....
* ....
* ....

personal

* ....
* ....
* ....
* ....
* ....
* ....
* ....
* ....
* ....

career

* ....
* ....
* ....
* ....
* ....
* ....
* ....
* ....
* ....
* ....

health

* ....
* ....
* ....
* ....
* ....
* ....
* ....
* ....
* ....
* ....

ONE GOAL.
COUNTLESS WAYS TO GET THERE.

When we encounter obstacles, trying to reach our goals can seem daunting. The trouble is compounded when we become fixated on a specific path to our goal, assuming that it's the only right way. In truth, there are an endless number of possible paths to our destination. The journey to achievement is like the exciting challenge of a game: we strategize from among countless routes and search for detours around the pieces that obstruct our path. The possibilities are without limit, and if we keep searching, we'll find creative new routes to our destination. We always have the freedom, privilege, and responsibility to make the best choices we can, no matter what blocks our way.

Whenever the path we are on is blocked, we always have two basic alternative plans to choose from to reach our dreams: we can branch off and take a completely new route, or we can start over from the beginning. Either way, we can get off to a strong start by creating a new life plan or updating the one we already have.

angel tip

In difficult times, time and effort will steadily work
their charm to change and improve the situation.
Difficult periods in life won't usually last much more
than a year. Have patience and persevere, and time
will open a path for you. In due course, the struggles
in your mind will fade, and you'll feel new hope rising
from within. Help and kindness will appear where there
used to be only obstacles.

create a life plan

Write down your objectives in life: short-term, mid-term, and long-term goals. If you're not ready to create a life plan yet, it's as effective to start by writing down goals that you can work toward immediately, in the near future, and in the more distant future. Be sure to make each goal authentic to the true self you discovered in chapter 1.

long-term goals

By .... *(10 years from today),*

I will have achieved these goals:

* ....
* ....
* ....
* ....
* ....
* ....
* ....
* ....
* ....
* ....
* ....
* ....
* ....
* ....

mid-term goals

To achieve these goals in 10 years, I will take these steps in the next 5 years:

* ....
* ....
* ....
* ....
* ....
* ....
* ....
* ....
* ....
* ....
* ....
* ....
* ....
* ....
* ....
* ....
* ....
* ....
* ....
* ....

short-term goals

To achieve my 5-year goals, here is what I will do during the coming year:

* ....
* ....
* ....
* ....
* ....
* ....
* ....
* ....
* ....
* ....
* ....
* ....
* ....
* ....
* ....
* ....
* ....
* ....
* ....
* ....
* ....

immediate goals

These are things I can do today to reach my 1-year goals:

* ....
* ....
* ....
* ....
* ....
* ....
* ....
* ....
* ....
* ....
* ....
* ....
* ....
* ....
* ....
* ....
* ....
* ....
* ....
* ....
* ....

MAKING DREAMS
COME TRUE

Reaching our goals and dreams is an important part of a happy life. We all do our best to set high ideals based on goodwill toward society and toward ourselves. But sometimes we get lost, can't see the road ahead, and suffer uncertainty. Everyone goes through a time when they aren't clear on what they should aspire to or where they're going in life. If you're at a dead end, don't know where to turn, or feel defeated or overcome, remember that prayer is a powerful tool that's always available to you. Prayer is a gift that has been given to all of us as our first and final way of realizing our sacred wishes. If our prayers are pure, heavenly beings will hear them. And if we need other people's help to actualize our dreams,

we can join hearts with our friends and pray together.

To manifest our wishes, we must set our minds on them and focus. It's important, when you pray, to rid your mind of negative attachments to physical or worldly things. So before you pray, make sure to consider your intentions and ensure that they align with a pure goal. Ask yourself, is this prayer compassionate toward myself, others, and the world? In this way, you will ensure that your prayers come from your true self, and you will develop great strength in avoiding unhealthy attachments.

The more time you spend visualizing your prayers in every detail, the more likely they are to manifest. When you close our eyes to focus quietly and see your dream play out vividly on the screen in your mind as if it's already happened, you engrave the image into your body and mind. The key to making your dreams a reality is to never doubt that they're already a reality.

A final tool for realizing our ideals is to trust in heaven. The wishes that we make in our hearts reach the other world instantly. Heavenly beings in the other world are always helping make our world a better place to live. When our goals align with their purpose, our guiding and guardian angels support us. Prayers bring us their help and protection. And the more clarity we give our wishes, the more our inner angels can give us the support we really need. So after you set intentions and then act on them, the next step is to make a regular practice of surrendering to the guidance of heavenly beings. If you're grounded in a pure purpose and taking daily action toward your goals, a path forward will open naturally and you'll move in the right direction. Patience and effort are key. When your prayers are answered, you must accept it with a humble heart and be grateful to all the heavenly beings who helped you. Then you can again ask for their support as you persevere toward further growth and contribution.

writing a prayer to *your inner angel*

Your inner angel leads you to what's best for you, protects you from what won't serve you, and guides you through the course of your life. When you take action for a noble cause or a higher ideal, your angel is the driving force behind you. Guided by this higher awareness, you're able to fulfill the greater missions that you are called to in life.

a prayer for dreams

Who would you like to be? How would you like to write the story of your life? In what ways can you offer the world more humility, kindness, and gratitude?

Answer the following questions, and after you've answered them, read them through. By reading your answers through, you create one long prayer for reaching your dreams and goals.

Choose one of your top goals from the "Create a Life Plan" exercise, and write a prayer to your inner angel asking for assistance or guidance in reaching it.

Dear inner angel,

My goal is ....

....

....

....

....

....

....

....

....

....

....

....

What is your plan of action for achieving your goal?

My plan of action is ....

....

....

....

....

....

....

....

....

....

....

....

....

....

....

....

....

....

....

....

....

....

....

....

....

What active "I am…" statements can you make about where you are on the path toward your goal? For example, "I am in the process of…" or "I am working toward being/becoming/earning/learning…"

I am ....

....

....

....

....

....

....

....

....

....

....

....

....

....

....

....

....

....

....

....

....

What practices can you put in place to support your goal? For instance, will you enlist the help of others so they know how to support you? Will you practice a daily visualization, prayer, or action? Describe your practices as specifically as you can.

To support my goal, I will ....

....

....

....

....

....

....

....

....

....

....

....

....

....

....

....

....

....

How will you incorporate your intention into your daily life? For instance, will you practice visualizing it daily or weekly? Where, when, and how often will you do this? Will you regularly review what you've written in your journal about your goals, dreams, and life plan?

To incorporate my intention into my daily life, I will ....

....
....
....
....
....
....
....
....
....
....
....
....
....
....
....
....
....
....
....
....

What things in your life are in conflict with your goal? What choices can you make to support your goal in your daily life?

To support my goal, I choose to ....

....

....

....

....

....

....

....

....

....

....

....

....

....

....

....

*My prayer of gratitude comes from my true self,
of a humble and selfless heart.*

*Thank you, inner angel, for helping me
become the best I can be.*

What positive changes have you seen since you accepted your invitation and began the spiritual journey to a happier you?

....
....
....
....
....
....
....
....
....
....
....
....
....
....
....
....
....
....
....
....
....
....

references

The following is a list of books written by Ryuho Okawa that have been used as references for *Invitation to Happiness* and that are available for purchase in the United States.

An Unshakable Mind: *How to Overcome Life's Difficulties*

The Challenge of the Mind: *A Practical Approach to the Essential Buddhist Teaching of Karma*

Change Your Life, Change the World: *A Spiritual Guide to Living Now*

Invincible Thinking: *There Is No Such Thing As Defeat*

The Laws of Great Enlightenment: *Always Walk with Buddha*

The Laws of Happiness: *The Four Principles for a Successful Life*

The Laws of Invincible Leadership: *How to Keep on Succeeding*

The Laws of Perseverance: *Reversing Your Common Sense*

The Laws of the Sun: *One Source, One Planet, One People*

Love, Nurture, and Forgive: *A Handbook to Add a New Richness to Your life*

The Moment of Truth: *Become A Living Angel Today*

The Nine Dimensions: *Unveiling the Laws of Eternity*

The Origin of Love: *On the Beauty of Compassion*

The Philosophy of Progress: *Higher Thinking for Developing Infinite Prosperity*

The Science of Happiness: *10 Principles for Manifesting Your Divine Nature*

Spiritual World 101: *A Guide to a Spiritually Happy Life*

The Starting Point of Happiness: *A Practical and Intuitive Guide to Discovering Love, Wisdom, and Faith*

This list does not include titles that had not yet been translated into English by the time *Invitation to Happiness* was published. New titles are continually being added. Be sure to visit okawabooks.com for the most updated list of books by Ryuho Okawa.

about the author

RYUHO OKAWA is a renowned spiritual thinker, leader, and author in Japan with a simple goal: to help people find true happiness and create a better world. To date, Okawa's books have sold over 100 million copies worldwide and been translated into 27 languages. His books address vital issues such as how our thoughts influence reality, the nature of love, and the path to enlightenment.

In 1986, Okawa founded Happy Science as a spiritual movement dedicated to bringing greater happiness to humankind by uniting religions and cultures to live in harmony. Happy Science has grown rapidly from its beginnings in Japan to a worldwide organization. The spiritual workshops Happy Science offers are open to people of all faiths and walks of life and are rooted in the same simple principles of happiness that inspired Okawa's own spiritual awakening. Okawa is compassionately committed to the spiritual growth of others; in addition to writing and publishing books, he continues to give talks around the world.

about happy science

Happy Science is a global movement that empowers individuals to find purpose and spiritual happiness and to share that happiness with their families, societies, and the world. With more than twelve million members around the world, Happy Science aims to increase awareness of spiritual truths and expand our capacity for love, compassion, and joy so that together we can create the kind of world we all wish to live in.

Activities at Happy Science are based on the Principles of Happiness (Love, Wisdom, Self-Reflection, and Progress). These principles embrace worldwide philosophies and beliefs, transcending boundaries of culture and religions.

Love teaches us to give ourselves freely without expecting anything in return; it encompasses giving, nurturing, and forgiving.

Wisdom leads us to the insights of spiritual truths and opens us to the true meaning of life and the will of God (the universe, the highest power, Buddha).

Self-reflection brings a mindful, nonjudgmental lens to our thoughts and actions to help us find our truest selves—the essence of our souls—and deepen our connection to the highest power. It helps us attain a clean and peaceful mind and leads us to the right life path.

Progress emphasizes the positive, dynamic aspects of our spiritual growth— actions we can take to manifest and spread happiness around the world. It's a path that not only expands our soul growth, but also furthers the collective potential of the world we live in.

programs and events

The doors of Happy Science are open to all. We offer a variety of programs and events, including self-exploration and self-growth programs, spiritual seminars, meditation and contemplation sessions, study groups, and book events.

Our programs are designed to:

* Deepen your understanding of your purpose and meaning in life
* Improve your relationships and increase your capacity to love unconditionally
* Attain peace of mind, decrease anxiety and stress, and feel positive
* Gain deeper insights and broader perspective on the world
* Learn how to overcome life's challenges
* And much more!

For more information, visit our website at happyscience-na.org or happy-science.org.

international seminars

Each year, friends from all over the world join our international seminars, held at our faith centers in Japan. Different programs are offered each year and cover a wide variety of topics, including improving relationships, practicing the Eightfold Path to enlightenment, and loving yourself, to name just a few.

happy science monthly

Our monthly publication covers the latest featured lectures, members' life-changing experiences and other news from members around the world, book reviews, and many other topics. Downloadable PDF files are available at happy-science.org. Copies and back issues in Portuguese, Chinese, and other languages are available upon request.

contact information

Happy Science is a worldwide organization with faith centers around the globe. For a comprehensive list of centers, visit the worldwide directory at www.happy-science.org. The following are some of the many Happy Science locations.

UNITED STATES AND CANADA

New York
79 Franklin Street
New York, NY 10013
Phone: 212-343-7972
Fax: 212-343-7973
Email: ny@happy-science.org
website: newyork.happyscience-na.org

Los Angeles
1590 E. Del Mar Blvd.
Pasadena, CA 91106
Phone: 626-395-7775
Fax: 626-395-7776
Email: la@happy-science.org
website: losangeles.happyscience-na.org

San Diego
Email: sandiego@happy-science.org

San Francisco
525 Clinton Street
Redwood City, CA 94062
Phone/Fax: 650-363-2777
Email: sf@happy-science.org
website: sanfrancisco.happyscience-na.org

Florida
12210 N 56th Street
Tampa, FL 33617
Phone:813-914-7771
Fax: 813-914-7710
Email: florida@happy-science.org
website: florida.happyscience-na.org

New Jersey
725 River Road, Suite 200
Edgewater, NJ 07025
Phone: 201-313-0127
Fax: 201-313-0120
Email: nj@happy-science.org
website: newjersey.happyscience-na.org

Atlanta
1874 Piedmont Ave. NE
Suite 360-C
Atlanta, GA 30324
Phone: 404-892-7770
Email: atlanta@happy-science.org
website: atlanta.happyscience-na.org

Hawaii

1221 Kapiolani Blvd., Suite 920
Honolulu, HI 96814
Phone: 808-591-9772
Fax: 808-591-9776
Email: hi@happy-science.org
website: hawaii.happyscience-na.org

Kauai

4504 Kukui Street
Dragon Building Suite 21
P. O. Box 1060
Kapaa, HI 96746
Phone: 808-822-7007
Fax: 808-822-6007
Email: kauai-hi@happy-science.org
website: www.happyscience-kauai.org

Toronto

323 College Street,
Toronto, ON M5T 1S2
Canada
Phone/Fax: 1-416-901-3747
Email: toronto@happy-science.org
website: happyscience-na.org

Vancouver

#212-2609 East 49th Avenue
Vancouver, V5S 1J9
Canada
Phone: 1-604-437-7735
Fax: 1-604-437-7764
Email: vancouver@happy-science.org
website: happyscience-na.org

INTERNATIONAL

Tokyo

1-6-7 Togoshi
Shinagawa, Tokyo, 142-0041
Japan
Phone: 81-3-6384-5770
Fax: 81-3-6384-5776
Email: tokyo@happy-science.org
website: happy-science.org

London

3 Margaret Street,
London, W1W 8RE
United Kingdom
Phone: 44-20-7323-9255
Fax: 44-20-7323-9344
Email: eu@happy-science.org
website: www.happyscience-uk.org

Sydney

516 Pacific Hwy
Lane Cove North,
2066 NSW
Australia
Phone: 61-2-9411-2877
Fax: 61-2-9411-2822
Email: aus@happy-science.org
website: www.happyscience.org.au

Brazil Headquarters

Rua. Domingos de Morais 1154,
Vila Mariana, Sao Paulo, CEP 04009-
002
Brazil
Phone: 55-11-5088-3800
Fax: 55-11-5088-3806
Email: sp@happy-science.org
website: www.cienciadafelicidade.com.br

Seoul
162-17 Sadang3-dong
Dongjak-gu, Seoul, Korea
Phone: 82-2-3478-8777
Fax: 82-2-3478-9777
Email: korea@happy-science.org
website: www.happyscience-korea.org

Taipei
No. 89, Lane 155, Dunhua N. Road
Songshan District
Taipei City 105
Taiwan
Phone: 886-2-2719-9377
Fax: 886-2-2719-5570
Email: taiwan@happy-science.org
website: www.happyscience-tw.org

Kathmandu
Sitapaila -15 kimdol
Ward no -15 Kathmandu
Nepal
Phone: 97-714-272931
Email: nepal@happy-science.org

Uganda
Plot 877 Rubaga Road Kampala
P.O. Box 34130
Kampala, Uganda
Phone: 256-78-4728-601
Email: uganda@happy-science.org
website: www.happyscience-uganda.org

about IRH press

Founded in 1987, IRH Press is the publishing, broadcast, and film production division of Happy Science. IRH Press currently has offices in Tokyo, New York, Sao Paulo, and Mumbai. The press publishes religious and spiritual books, journals, and magazines and also operates broadcast and film production enterprises. For more information, visit OkawaBooks.com.